Language Builders

Vivian and Victor Learn about
VERBS

by Ann Malaspina
illustrated by Linda Prater

Content Consultant
Roxanne Owens
Associate Professor, Elementary Reading
DePaul University

NORWOOD HOUSE PRESS
CHICAGO, ILLINOIS

Norwood House Press
P.O. Box 316598
Chicago, Illinois 60631
For information regarding Norwood House Press, please visit our website at:
www.norwoodhousepress.com or call 866-565-2900.

Editor: Arnold Ringstad
Designer: Jake Nordby
Project Management: Red Line Editorial

Library of Congress Cataloging-in-Publication Data
Malaspina, Ann, 1957-
  Vivian and Victor learn about verbs / by Ann Malaspina ; illustrated by Linda Prater.
      p. cm.
   Includes bibliographical references.
   Summary: "Vivian and Victor learn about verbs while they prepare for a race in the park. Concepts include: basic definition and usage of verbs; action and being verbs; past, present, and future tense; progressive tense; irregular verbs; main verbs; and helping verbs. Activities in the back help reinforce text concepts. Includes glossary and additional resources"-- Provided by publisher.
   ISBN 978-1-59953-667-5 (library edition : alk. paper) -- ISBN 978-1-60357-727-4 (ebook)
   1. English language--Verb--Juvenile literature. 2. English language--Parts of speech--Juvenile literature. 3. Running races--Juvenile literature. I. Prater, Linda, illustrator. II. Title.
   PE1271.M33 2015
   428.1--dc22
                                                         2014030327

©2015 by Norwood House Press.
All rights reserved.
No part of this book may be reproduced without written permission from the publisher.
Manufactured in the United States of America in North Mankato, Minnesota.
262N—122014

Time for Action

I'm exhausted! I just ran five times around the block. I'm training for the Race in the Park on Friday. I want to surprise my friend Victor at the starting line. He's the best runner at school. Victor thinks I can't run, but I'll prove him wrong.

Our teacher, Mr. Gully, tells us that words like <u>read</u>, <u>write</u>, and <u>watch</u> are action verbs. <u>Run</u> is also an action verb. I guess some action verbs have more action than others. Action verbs aren't the only kind of verbs, though. You can't write a sentence without a verb, so that makes all verbs important.

The Race in the Park is the same day as Mr. Gully's test on verbs. I have three things to do this week. First, I'll train for the race. Second, I'll keep it a secret from Victor. And third, I'll learn everything I can about verbs. Get ready for a big week!

By Vivian, age 9

Vivian jogged down the path in the park. Her dog, Rainbow, trotted beside her. The sun was hot, and they were getting tired.

Around the bend, they almost crashed into Victor. He was sprinting the other way.

"Vivian! What are you doing here?" Victor asked. She was training for the Race in the Park, but Vivian didn't want to tell Victor. He was the captain of the school track team. He might laugh at her.

"I'm heading home to study for Mr. Gully's verb test tomorrow," she said, catching her breath.

"I like **action** verbs. They tell what the subject of the sentence is doing," said Victor. He did ten jumping jacks and stretched his legs.

"I like them, too," said Vivian, touching her toes. "Especially action verbs like *exercise*, *train*, and *win*."

"You do?" Victor pointed at her running shoes. "Why are you wearing those? You never wear running shoes!" Vivian usually wore fancy shoes or sandals. She wasn't on a sports team. She was in the film club and wrote for the school newspaper.

Vivian changed the subject. "I'm hungry. Do you want an Italian ice?"

The ice cream man in the playground sold them a raspberry ice and a lemon ice. They sat on the swings, eating their delicious treats. "Let's talk about verbs. Do you understand **linking** verbs?" asked Vivian.

"Linking verbs connect a subject with a word that gives information about the subject," said Victor. "They're also called **being** verbs. Words like *is*, *seem*, or *feel* are linking verbs."

"I think I understand," said Vivian. "Victor *is* sweating. Vivian *seems* very smart! *Is* and *seem* are linking verbs. They help to describe us."

"Maybe it's the other way around. Vivian is sweating and Victor seems very smart!" teased Victor.

Rainbow chased a squirrel up a tree. "Come here, Rainbow!" Vivian called.

"I remember something Mr. Gully told us. The verb always has to agree with the noun," Victor said.

"Let's figure out what he meant by that," said Vivian.

Victor got off the swing and threw a stick to Rainbow. Vivian thought of a sentence. "Rainbow *chases* a stick," she said.

They watched as another dog joined in. "Two dogs *chase* a stick," Vivian added. "The verb ending changes when the subject is plural."

"*Chases* and *chase*," said Victor. "I think I get it!" The sun was starting to set. "I had better go. I want to run another half mile," said Victor.

Vivian waited until Victor disappeared down the path. Then she and Rainbow ran all the way home.

That night, Victor phoned Vivian. "I'm still curious. Why were you wearing running shoes in the park this afternoon?" he asked.

Vivian ignored his question. "I'm trying to study for the test."

"Actually, I have a verb question," said Victor. "Do verbs have to be about something I'm doing right now?"

"No, verbs can be about actions in the past, present, or **future**," said Vivian. "It's all about **verb tense**."

"Wow, the future! Verbs can travel through time?" Victor asked.

"Sort of. Verbs in the future tense tell an action that is going to happen," said Vivian. "You add the verb *will* to most verbs to make the future tense. I *will* get an A on the test tomorrow."

"You wish!" Victor said. "So, that covers stuff in the future. Now how about things in the past? I know that verbs in the past tense tell about an action that already happened. But how do you make a verb past tense?"

"For most verbs, you add a *–d* or *–ed* to make them past tense," said Vivian. "My dad *cooks* lasagna all the time. Two days ago, my dad *cooked* lasagna. He *cooked* it again yesterday."

"That's a lot of lasagna! You aren't eating lots of food to get energy for a race, are you?" asked Victor.

"Don't forget about what Mr. Gully said about **irregular** verbs," Vivian said. She looked down at her notes from class. "Irregular verbs don't add *–d* or *–ed* in the past tense. Instead, the word's spelling changes. *Begin*, *break*, *fly*, and *do* are a few irregular verbs. They turn into *began*, *broke*, *flew*, and *did*."

Irregular Verbs
- don't add –d or –ed to make past tense
- change spelling

Present	Past
begin	began
break	broke
	flew

After Victor hung up, Vivian remembered something else. Some irregular verbs, such as *read* and *hit*, stay the same in different tenses. I *hit* the baseball last week, and I *hit* the baseball today.

The next day, Victor and Vivian arrived at school early. She wore running shoes and green sweatpants. Green was her lucky color.

Vivian sat next to Victor in Mr. Gully's class. She told Victor about the irregular verbs that don't change. "I already know about them," said Victor. "Why are you wearing sweatpants?"

Vivian pretended not to hear. "Mr. Gully, I am trying to understand main verbs and helping verbs," she said. "I don't understand the difference."

Mr. Gully said, "Good question! Let's all review this before the test." He wrote a sentence on the chalkboard: "The main verb tells the action."

Then he said, "Remember, the helping verb is important, too. It helps us understand what the sentence means. Who can tell me how main verbs and helping verbs work together?"

Victor raised his hand, and Mr. Gully called on him. "The helping verb always comes before the main verb," said Victor. "Victor *could win* the race. *Could* is the helping verb. *Win* is the main verb."

Vivian just hoped she would finish the race, let alone win!

"Sounds like you have it covered," said Mr. Gully. "Don't forget the **progressive** tense. Remember to look for the *–ing* ending. Vivian, can you tell me what verbs in the progressive tense do?"

Vivian responded right away. "A verb in the progressive tense shows an action that happens over time," she said. "It can be in the past, present, or future."

"I feel like we've been *studying* verbs forever!" whispered Victor to Vivian.

"Right!" Mr. Gully said. "I think we're ready to test your knowledge." He began handing out the test. "Good luck, everyone!" he said.

The test wasn't too hard. Studying had paid off. After it was over, Victor gave Vivian a high five in the hall outside the classroom. "Are you going to watch the race later?" asked Victor.

Vivian bit her lip and didn't say anything. Vivian thought secrets were very hard to keep.

The race was at 4 o'clock. The park was full of people. At the starting line, Vivian bent down to tie her laces. "Vivian!" She heard Victor's voice. "What are you doing here?"

"I'm *planning* to run the race," she said, standing up. "That's progressive tense!"

Instead of laughing at her, Victor said, "Good luck!"

"Thanks. You, too!" she replied.

The starting whistle blew. Victor and Vivian both started in the middle of the pack. Victor pulled ahead quickly. Vivian kept up with many of the runners.

Twenty-three minutes later, Vivian crossed the finish line. Victor cheered from the sidelines. "Congratulations! You finished in the top half," he said. "You should join the track team!"

Vivian and Victor clapped as the other

familiar. Their teacher struggled to cross the finish line. "If I'm going to teach verbs, I need to be active," said Mr. Gully, huffing and puffing.

Victor and Vivian called out to their teacher, "Good job, Mr. Gully!"

Know Your Verbs

Verbs make things happen. Every sentence needs at least one verb. Some verbs show action. Other verbs link the subject with more information about the subject. They're called linking or being verbs.

Verbs change in the past, present, and future. Regular verbs are easy to change to the past tense. You just add a –d or –ed. "I will *play* the drums today" becomes "I *played* the drums yesterday." Most irregular verbs change spelling. Some stay the same. Look at these irregular verbs: *throw*, *ride*, *sweep*, and *shut*. Can you make them past tense?

Main verbs tell the action in the sentence. Helping verbs come before the main verb. Vinny *was practicing* his tuba. *Was* is the helping verb. *Practicing* is the main verb.

Find the verbs in these sentences. Tell whether they are action or linking verbs. Are they in the past, present, or future tense? Are they main verbs or helping verbs? Look for progressive verbs, too. Remember, those have an *–ing* ending. Which sentence has three verbs?

> Victor will stretch his legs before the big race.
>
> The ice cream man sells raspberry ice.
>
> Vivian is keeping a secret.

Two dogs chased a stick.

Vivian and Victor studied for a test, ate dinner, and ran a race.

Mr. Gully is planning to practice running some more.

Writing Activity

Action verbs give the subject something to do. They give energy and meaning to sentences. Action verbs make a person parachute out of a plane and a race car speed around the track. But all action verbs aren't equal. Some action verbs are boring. Others are more exciting. Think about *walk* versus *shuffle*, *whisper* versus *hiss*, and *laugh* versus *guffaw*. Which verbs would you rather read in a story?

Now write a story about a contest you participated in. Use lots of verbs. After you write a first draft, circle all the verbs. For every verb, write a second verb that is more exciting. Exciting verbs will make your sentences come alive. They may make people more interested in reading what you write.

Glossary

action: something done.

being: existing.

future: coming after the present.

irregular: not normal or usual.

linking: connecting.

progressive: an ongoing action.

verb tense: when a verb takes place in time.

For More Information

Books

Ganeri, Anita. *Action Words: Verbs*. Chicago: Heinemann Library, 2012.

TIME for Kids: Grammar Rules! New York: Time Home Entertainment, 2013.

Websites

Mrs. Warner's Fourth Grade Classroom
http://mrswarnerarlington.weebly.com/verbs.html
This website has links to games and worksheets about verbs.

Turtle Diary
http://www.turtlediary.com/kids-games/ela-topics/verb-games.html
Play fun games to practice verbs.

About the Author

Ann Malaspina is the author of many books for children. She likes to brainstorm for exciting verbs. She also enjoys writing poems and stories.